t lights **five** books of the torah
directions in the world **thirteen**
forty days and **forty** nights two
elve tribes **three** shabbos meals
four sons **seventy** nations of the
commandments **four** directions
t ways to explain the torah **six**
r **ten** days of rep... **seven**
ne jewish nation **twelve** tribes
ght days of chanukah **four** sons
t lights **five** books of the torah
ation **six hundred and thirteen**
e torah **ten** days of repentance
thirteen commandments **eight**
forty nights **forty-nine** days of
ls **seventy** nations of the world
five megillos **one** jewish nation

D1717056

WHO KNOWS ONE?

a book of Jewish numbers

written by Yaffa Ganz

illustrated by
Harvey Klineman

 FELDHEIM PUBLISHERS Jerusalem/New York

First published 1981
ISBN 0-87306-285-X

Copyright © 1981 by
Yaffa Ganz and Harvey Klineman

Phototypeset at the Feldheim Press

Philipp Feldheim Inc.
96 East Broadway
New York, NY 10002

Feldheim Publishers Ltd
POB 6525 / Jerusalem, Israel

Printed in Israel

תורה צוה לנו משה מורשה קהילת יעקב

For
Seffy and Noa
and Shani and Yedidya
and all the
tinokos
shel beis rabban—
Jewish children
who learn the Torah.

All Hebrew words appear in *italics* and are explained
either in the text or in the glossary at the end of the book.

WHO KNOWS ONE?

We all know ONE.
God is ONE.
He made everyone and everything,
and He watches over us all the time.
Every day we say

שְׁמַע יִשְׂרָאֵל ה׳ אֱלֹקֵינוּ ה׳ אֶחָד.

HEAR O ISRAEL,
THE LORD OUR GOD,
THE LORD IS ONE.

There is ONE God, ONE Torah, ONE Jewish nation, and ONE Land of Israel.

Who knows TWO Do you?

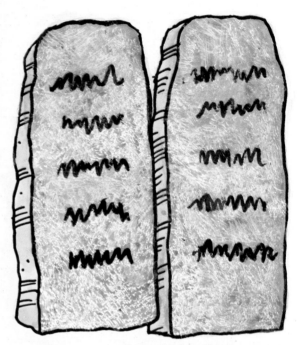

TWO are the *luchos habris*— the TWO tablets that *Moshe Rabbeinu* brought down from *Har Sinai*.

We put *lechem mishneh*— TWO *challos*— on the table each *Shabbos*.

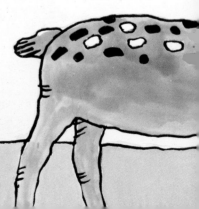

God made
TWO great lights—
the sun and the moon—
on the fourth day of
creation.

And the animals in Noach's ark all came in PAIRS!

Who knows

3

WHO KNOWS THREE?
THREE are the *avos*—
the Fathers of the Jewish people—
Avraham, Yitzchak and Yaakov.

We pray
THREE times a day—
shacharis in the morning,
minchah in the afternoon,
and *maariv* in the evening.

The *shofar* makes
THREE different sound
on *Rosh Hashanah*—

We eat THREE
special *Shabbos* meals—
shalosh seudos.

TEKIAH

SHEVARIM

TRUAH

The Jews went up to the *beis hamikdash* in Jerusalem
THREE times a year— *Pesach*, *Shavuos* and *Sukkos*.

On *motza'ei shabbos*
we say *havdalah*
when we see
THREE stars
in the sky.

Who knows FOUR?

There are lots of things to tell about the number FOUR!

Sarah, Rivkah, Rachel and Leah are the FOUR *imahos*—the Mothers of the Jewish people.

At the *seder* we ask FOUR questions, drink FOUR cups of wine, and talk about the FOUR sons.

Tzitzis are put on clothes which have FOUR corners.

There are FOUR directions in the world— *tzafon* is north; *darom* is south; *mizrach* is east; and *maarav* is west. We face *mizrach* when we pray because *Eretz Yisrael* is in the east.

צפון
N

מערב
W

מזרח
E

דרום
S

FOUR rivers flowed out of *gan eden*. Do you know their names? The *Pishon*, the *Gichon*, the *Chidekel* and the *Peras*.

On *Sukkos*, we make a blessing on the *arba'ah minim*— FOUR types of plants— the *lulav*, *esrog*, *hadas* and *aravah*.

ד

Who knows FIVE?

Many of the books in the *Tanach* come in FIVES.

There are
chamishah chumshei Torah—
FIVE books of the Torah.
Their names are
Bereishis, Shemos, Vayikra,
Bamidbar, and *Devarim.*

David Hamelech wrote
FIVE books of *Tehillim*—
one book of *Tehillim*
for each of the
FIVE books in the Torah.

There are FIVE *megillos*—
Ruth, Esther, Koheles,
Shir Hashirim and *Eicha.*
Do you remember
when each one is read?

Who knows SIX?

I know SIX!

The world was created in SIX days.

The SIX books
of the *Mishnah*—
*Zeraim, Moed,
Nashim, Nezikin,
Kodashim* and
Taharos—
explain the laws
of the Torah.

We put SIX things
on the *seder* plate—
beitzah, zeroah, and *maror;
karpas, charoses,* and *chazeres.*

Golden lions
and eagles
stood on the SIX steps
leading up to
Shlomo Hamelech's throne.

Shabbos is the SEVENTH day of the week.

Who knows SEVEN?

The *menorah* in the *beis hamikdash* had SEVEN branches.

In *Eretz Yisrael*, every SEVENTH year is a *shmittah* year—a Sabbath year for the land.

The Land of Israel is blessed with SEVEN types of fruits— *shivah minim*— wheat, barley, grapes, figs, pomegranates, olives and dates.

We say *sheva brachos*— SEVEN blessings— for every bride and groom.

When SEVEN *kohanim* blew SEVEN *shofaros* and the Jews marched SEVEN times round, the walls of the city of Jericho crumbled and fell.

Who knows EIGHT?

EIGHT means *Chanukah*!

EIGHT days of miracles and EIGHT days of light!

EIGHT means *bris milah*. A Jewish boy is circumcised and given his Hebrew name when he is only EIGHT days old.

EIGHT means *Shmini Atzeres*— an extra, EIGHTH day of rejoicing after the holiday of *Sukkos*.

Who knows NINE?

Tishah b'Av— the NINTH day of the month of Av —is an unhappy day for the Jewish people. Both the first and the second *batei mikdash* were destroyed on that day.

But NINE is a happy number too. A tiny baby grows inside its mother for NINE months until it is finally born!

Who knows TEN?

There were TEN generations from Adam to Noach, and TEN generations from Noach to Avraham.

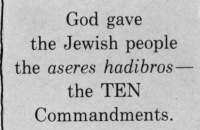
God gave
the Jewish people
the *aseres hadibros*—
the TEN
Commandments.

TEN men make a *minyan*.
A *minyan* prays together
in the synagogue.

A Jew gives
maaser—a TENTH
of his earnings—
to *tzedakah*.

There are

10

days of repentance—
aseres y'mei teshuvah—
between *Rosh Hashanah*
and *Yom Kippur*.

Who knows 12

Yaakov Avinu had TWELVE sons who were the heads of the TWELVE tribes of Israel.

REUVEN

SHIMON

LEVI

YEHUDAH

YISSACHAR

ZEVULUN

NAFTALI

GAD

DAN

ASHER

YOSEF

BINYAMIN

There are
TWELVE
months in a year,
and a group of stars in the
sky for each one—
TWELVE
in all.

ADAR NISSAN IYYAR SIVAN TAMMUZ AV ELUL TISHREY CHESHVAN KISLEV TEVES SHEVAT

Jewish girls
become *bas mitzvah*
when they are
TWELVE
years old.

Who knows THIRTEEN?

A Hebrew leap year has THIRTEEN months instead of twelve.

ADAR I 'א אדר
1 2 3 4 5 6
7 8 9 10 11 12 13
14 15 16 17 18 19 20
21 22 23 24 25 26 27
28 29

Jewish boys become *bar mitzvah* when they are THIRTEEN years old.

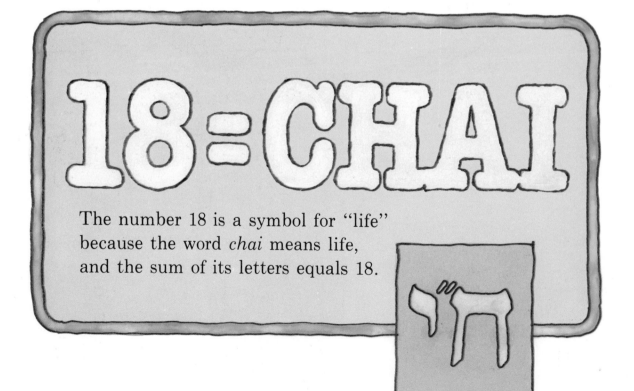

18 = CHAI

The number 18 is a symbol for "life" because the word *chai* means life, and the sum of its letters equals 18.

39

Bnei Yisrael did 39 different kinds of work while they were building the *mishkan*.

These are the 39 kinds of work we are not allowed to do on the Sabbath.

Moshe Rabbeinu
went up to *Har Sinai*
for 40 days and
40 nights.

The Jewish people wandered in the desert for 40 yea

David Hamelech was
King of Israel for 40 years,
and his son Shlomo ruled for
40 years after him.

Rabbi Akiva began to learn
the Torah when he was 40 years old.

There are 49 days
between *Pesach* and *Shavuos*.
These are the 49 days of
sfiras haOmer—counting the *Omer*.

היום
48
בעומר

47

46

45

44

70 Jews—
Yaakov Avinu,
his twelve sons,
and their families—
went down to
the land of Egypt.

70 elders helped Moshe teach
the Torah to the Jewish people.

The 70 nations
of the world spoke
70 different languages.
The rabbis of
the *sanhedrin*
understood them all.

The Jews began to build
the second *beis hamikdash*
exactly 70 years after the
first *beis hamikdash* was destroyed.

The Torah
can be
explained
in 70
different ways.

120

Moshe Rabbeinu
lived for 120 years.
That's why we say,
"May you live to be 120!"

קכ״

613

The Torah has
taryag mitzvos—
613 commandments.

(The Hebrew letters *taryag* equal the number 613.)

Who knows...

a. how long the Jews were in Egypt?

b. how many books are in the *Tanach*?

c. when we light the *Shabbos* candles?

d. how many days are in a Hebrew month?

e. another number for the 18th of Iyar?

f. how many clothes the *kohein gadol* wore?

g. how often we say a blessing on the sun?

h. when we celebrate the New Year for Trees?

i. how many prophets are mentioned in the *Tanach*?

j. the number of blessings a Jew should say each day?

k. when *Moshe Rabbeinu*'s birthday was? when he died?

l. how many blessings are in the *shemoneh esrey*?

---

a. Two hundred and ten years.

b. Twenty-four books.

c. At least eighteen minutes before sunset.

d. Either twenty-nine or thirty days.

e. Lag BaOmer—the 33rd day in the Omer.

f. Eight different pieces of clothing.

g. Once every twenty-eight years.

h. On Tu B'Shvat—the 15th of Shvat.

i. Forty-eight.

j. One hundred.

k. Both dates are the 7th of Adar.

l. Not eighteen but nineteen. One blessing was added later on.

a glossary of

Aravah: willow leaves

Bamidbar: the fourth book in the Torah (Numbers)

Bar Mitzvah: a Jewish boy age 13 or over

Bas Mitzvah: a Jewish girl age 12 or over

Beis Hamikdash (batei mikdash): the Holy Temple in Jerusalem

Beitzah: a hard-boiled egg used on the Passover *seder* plate

Bereishis: the first book in the Torah (Genesis)

Bnei Yisrael: the Children of Israel, the Jewish people

Challah (challos): a loaf of braided white bread for the Sabbath

Charoses: chopped nuts, apples and wine; eaten during the Passover *seder*

Chazeres: bitter herbs placed on the Passover *seder* plate

David Hamelech: King David

Devarim: the fifth book in the Torah (Deuteronomy)

Eicha: one of the five Scrolls in the Bible (Lamentations); written by
the prophet Jeremiah

Eretz Yisrael: the Land of Israel

Esrog: a citron

Gan Eden: the Garden of Eden

Hadas: leaves from the myrtle bush

Havdalah: the ceremony to end the Sabbath

Karpas: a vegetable dipped in salt water during the Passover *seder*

Kohein (kohanim): a descendant of the priestly tribe

Koheles: one of the five Scrolls in the Bible (Ecclesiastes); written by King Solomo

Lulav: palm leaves

Maror: bitter herbs eaten during the Passover *seder*

Megillos: the five books in the Bible called the Scrolls

Menorah: a candelabra

Minyan: a group of ten men or boys above the age of 13

Mishkan: the Tabernacle, where the Holy Ark was kept during the forty years
wandering in the desert

Hebrew words

Mishnah: the Oral Law of the Torah

Moshe Rabbeinu: Moses our teacher

Motza'ei Shabbos: the evening after the Sabbath day

Omer: an offering of barley from the spring harvest, brought to the *beis hamikdash* on the second day of Passover

Pesach: Passover; the Festival of Freedom from slavery in Egypt

Rosh HaShanah: the New Year holiday

Sanhedrin: Supreme Court of seventy-one rabbis in the time of the *beis hamikdash*

Seder: the festive meal on the first and second nights of Passover

Shabbos: the Sabbath day

Shavuos: the time of the Giving of the Torah and the Festival of the First Fruits

Shemos: the second book in the Torah (Exodus)

Shevarim: three short sounds on the *shofar*

Shir Hashirim: the Song of Songs, written by King Solomon

Shofar (shofaros): a ram's horn

Shlomo Hamelech: King Solomon

Sukkos: the holiday when we remember the forty years wandering in the desert and the gathering in of the crops in Eretz Yisrael

Tanach: the Bible

Tehillim: the Psalms of David

Tekiah: a long, continuous blow on the *shofar*

Teruah: nine very short blows on the *shofar*

Tzedakah: charity

Tzitzis: knotted fringes worn on four cornered clothing to remind us of the 613 commandments in the Torah. (The Hebrew letters *tzitzis* equal the number 600. The 5 knots and 8 strings in each corner equal 13).

Vayikra: the third book in the Torah (Leviticus)

Yaakov Avinu: our forefather Jacob

Yom Kippur: the Day of Repentance

Zeroah: a roasted bone used on the *seder* plate

Hebrew Numbers

THIS LETTER		THIS NUMBER	
ALEPH	א	1	ACHAS
BEIS	בּ	2	SHTAYIM
GIMEL	ג	3	SHALOSH
DALED	ד	4	ARBA
HEY	ה	5	CHAMEISH
VAV	ו	6	SHEISH
ZAYIN	ז	7	SHEVA
CHES	ח	8	SHMONEH
TES	ט	9	TEISHA
YUD	י	10	ESER
KAF	כּ	20	ESRIM
LAMED	ל	30	SHLOSHIM
MEM	מ	40	ARBA'IM
NUN	נ	50	CHAMISHIM
SAMECH	ס	60	SHISHIM
AYIN	ע	70	SHIV'IM
PEY	פּ	80	SHMONIM
TZADI	צ	90	TISH'IM
KUF	ק	100	MEAH
REISH	ר	200	MASAYIM
SHIN	שׁ	300	SHLOSH MEYOS
TAV	ת	400	ARBA MEYOS

eight days of chanukah two gr
ments three shabbos meals four
five megillos one jewish nation
seventy nations of the world tw
nations ten days of repentance
world six hundred and thirteen
sefiras ha'omer seventy differe
forty-nine days of sefiras ha'om
one land of israel five megillos
and forty nights twelve tribes
ten days of repentance two gre
nights five megillos one jewish
two great lights five books of th
sefiras ha'omer six hundred an
commandments forty days and
twelve tribes three shabbos me
eight days of chanukah four son